The Biography of Potatoes

Ellen Rodger

Crabtree Publishing Company
www.crabtreebooks.com

Crabtree Publishing Company

www.crabtreebooks.com

For Jimmy - Ellen

For Donovan , I only have 'eyes' for you -Love Samara

Coordinating editor: Ellen Rodger
Series editor: Carrie Gleason
Project editor: L. Michelle Nielsen
Editor: Adrianna Morganelli
Design and production coordinator: Rosie Gowsell
Production assistance and layout: Samara Parent
Art direction: Rob MacGregor
Scanning technician: Arlene Arch-Wilson
Photo research: Allison Napier
Prepress technician: Nancy Johnson

Photo Credits: Agripicture Images/Alamy: p. 9 (top); Blickwinkel/Alamy: p. 22 (top); Gary Cook/Alamy: p. 19 (bottom); Danita Delimont/Alamy: cover, p. 5 (bottom); Terry Donnelly/Alamy: p. 20 (bottom); Paul Glendell/Alamy: p. 27 (bottom); Jeff Greenberg/Alamy: p. 28 (bottom); Richard Levine/Alamy: p. 29 (top); Lordprice Collection/Alamy: p. 21; TB Photo Communications, Inc./Alamy: p. 9 (bottom); The Art Archive/Eileen Tweedy: p. 4 (left); Bibliotheque des Arts Decoratifs, Paris, France, Archives Charmet/The Bridgeman Art Library: p. 4 (right); Private Collection, Johnny Van Haeften Ltd., London/The Bridgeman Art Library: p. 16; Niall Benvie/Corbis: p. 26 (bottom); David Frazier/Corbis: p. 24; Jeremy Horner/Corbis: p. 7; James Marshall/Corbis: p. 25 (both); Kazuyoshi Nomachi/Corbis: p. 12; Reuters/Corbis: p. 13 (top); Stapleton Collection/Corbis: p. 19 (top); CP PHOTO/Charlottetown Guardian/Brian McInnis: p. 26 (middle left); The Granger Collection, New York: p. 14, p. 15 (bottom), p. 17, p. 22 (bottom); Jack K. Clark/The Image Works: p. 27 (top); Mary Evans Picture Library/The Image Works: p. 8 (top), p. 15 (top), p. 18 (bottom); NMPFT/SSPL/The Image Works: p. 29 (bottom); Ann Ronan Picture Library/HIP/The Image Works: p. 23 (top); Adam Tanner/The Image Works: p. 11 (top): North Wind/North Wind Picture Archives: p. 20 (top); Panos Pictures/G.M.B. Akash: p. 1; Nigel Cattlin/Photo Researchers, Inc.: p. 26 (top); David R. Frazier/Photo Researchers, Inc.: p. 10, p. 11 (top); Jerome Wexler/Photo Researchers, Inc.: p. 8 (bottom); REUTERS/Pilar Olivares: p. 31 (bottom); REUTERS/Rafiquar Rahman: p. 30. Other images from stock photo cd

Cartography: Jim Chernishenko: p. 6

Cover: Potatoes are cultivated throughout much of the world. This farmer from France is harvesting a field of potatoes.

Title page: These women are tilling a potato field in Nepal, a developing country in southwest Asia.

Contents page: Potato chip companies make millions of dollars a year selling the popular potato snack.

Library and Archives Canada Cataloguing in Publication

Rodger, Ellen
    The biography of potatoes / Ellen Rodger.

(How did that get here?)
Includes index.
ISBN 978-0-7787-2492-6 (bound)
ISBN 978-0-7787-2528-2 (pbk.)

    1. Potatoes--Juvenile literature. I. Title. II. Series.

SB211.P8R63 2007   j635'.21   C2007-900698-1

Library of Congress Cataloging-in-Publication Data

Rodger, Ellen.
    The Biography of potatoes / written by Ellen Rodger.
        p. cm. -- (How did that get here?)
    Includes index.
    ISBN-13: 978-0-7787-2492-6 (rlb)
    ISBN-10: 0-7787-2492-1 (rlb)
    ISBN-13: 978-0-7787-2528-2 (pb.)
    ISBN-10: 0-7787-2528-6 (pb.)
    1. Potatoes--Juvenile literature. I. Title. II. Series.

SB211.P8R63 2007
635'.21--dc22   2007003458

Crabtree Publishing Company

www.crabtreebooks.com   1-800-387-7650

Published in Canada
Crabtree Publishing
616 Welland Ave.
St. Catharines, ON
L2M 5V6

Published in the United States
Crabtree Publishing
PMB16A
350 Fifth Ave., Suite 3308
New York, NY 10118

Published in the United Kingdom
Crabtree Publishing
White Cross Mills
High Town, Lancaster
LA1 4XS

Published in Australia
Crabtree Publishing
386 Mt. Alexander Rd.
Ascot Vale (Melbourne)
VIC 3032

Contents

A Historic Vegetable

Hundreds of years ago, the potato was unknown to most of the world. It grew only in the **Andes Mountains** of South America. Today, it is hard to imagine a world without potatoes. For many people throughout the world, the potato is a food staple that grows easily in many climates and can be cooked and eaten a thousand different ways. The potato plant was taken from South America and introduced to Europe in the 1500s. At first, outside of South America, it was a food deemed fit only for pigs and peasants. Over time, the potato proved to be a very valuable vegetable, so **nutritious** that it has saved millions of lives over the course of history.

▸ *Potato plants have stems, leaves, and flowers that grow above ground, and roots, rhizomes, or underground stems, and potatoes, which grow underground.*

DOCTOR CARROT *guards your Health*

VIT·A

I'm an *Energy* Food !
Says 'POTATO PETE'

◂ *Advertisements from the 1940s promoted the benefits of vegetables, including potatoes, to people's health.*

Starch Rival

The potato is a round, lumpy vegetable that grows under the soil. It is the world's fourth largest crop, behind rice, wheat, and corn. Potatoes are hardy, which means that they can be grown in many different soils and climatic conditions. A small patch of potatoes also goes a long way, and can feed many people. Potatoes contain many minerals, vitamins, and starch, which makes them nutritious. Potato starch is a **carbohydrate** that the body breaks down and uses for energy. A person could survive on potatoes and little else because of the food energy potatoes produce.

(above right) A popular way to prepare potatoes is baked with a dollop of sour cream and chives.

(below) This woman is selling potatoes at a market in Peru, a country in South America. Potatoes originated and are still a staple there.

Food Staple

Potatoes are considered a staple food. A staple food is one that is often planted, grown, and harvested by the same people who consume, or eat them. All over the world, potatoes are grown in backyard patches or gardens as an everyday food. In some areas of the world, massive potato farms, which use expensive and sophisticated farm machinery, produce potato crops for **commercial** sale and use. The potatoes grown on these farms are sold in grocery stores and sent to **processors** to make products such as potato chips, frozen French fries, alcohol, starches, and even non-food products such as **biodegradable** forks and knives, and coatings for paper, which make paper products stronger.

A Home Worldwide

Scientists have traced the origin of the potato to a wild plant that grew in the South American country of Peru. Thousands of years ago, the ancient peoples of the Andes Mountains began to domesticate, or plant and farm, the wild potato. They grew potatoes on the Andes altiplano, which is a plateau, or area of flat land up in the mountains. Potatoes were farmed on terraces, which are steps or raised banks of soil built into the sides of mountains. Andean farmers developed and grew many kinds of potatoes, which were suited to the many different climate conditions that existed on the mountains.

Spanish Transport

In the mid-1500s, the Spanish came to **conquer** the lands and **plunder** the riches of South America. While Spanish conquistadors, or conquerors, were searching for gold in the Andes, they noticed the local farmers grew a low-lying plant as their main food crop. The Spanish were not very interested in the plant, and it took them many years to recognize its value. Nobody knows exactly how the first potatoes made it from the Andes to Spain, but potatoes were used in Spain by the 1570s, mainly as a food for the poor.

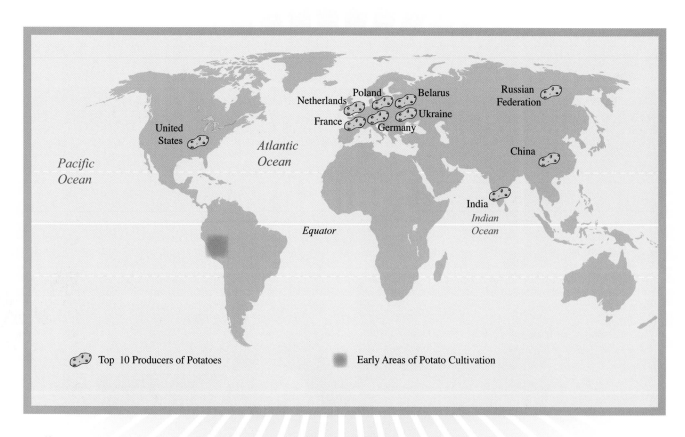

Different varieties of potatoes are suited to different climates and environments. Potatoes are grown in most regions in the world, including the tropics and temperate zones, or areas with mild temperatures.

Adaptable Potatoes

From Spain, over the next several hundred years, the potato spread throughout Europe, Asia, North America, the Middle East, and Africa. Today, potatoes are grown in almost every country in the world. Millions of tons of potatoes are commercially harvested every year. The potato has proven to be an adaptable food crop, with different varieties suited to different growing conditions. Potatoes are grown on the sides of mountains and at the ocean's edge in **tropical** countries, and in arid, or dry, countries. Many countries produce potatoes for domestic consumption, or sale inside the country. Potatoes are also exported, or sold to other countries, and used to make processed foods, such as potato chips.

South Americans used terrace farming to cultivate potatoes. The terraces stopped rainwater from flowing down the mountainside, allowing the crops to get enough water to grow.

How Potatoes Grow

Unlike many other plants, potatoes do not have seeds that can be scattered in a garden or field. Potatoes are grown from other potatoes, or what are commonly called "seed potatoes." Seed potatoes have sprouts that look like fat roots. The sprouts grow out of small indents, called eyes, in a potato's surface. When seed potatoes are planted, the sprouts develop roots. Small hairs on the potato's roots pull nutrients and water from the soil to feed the growing plant.

(right) Before motorized farming equipment was available, farmers did a lot of work by hand, including planting seed potatoes.

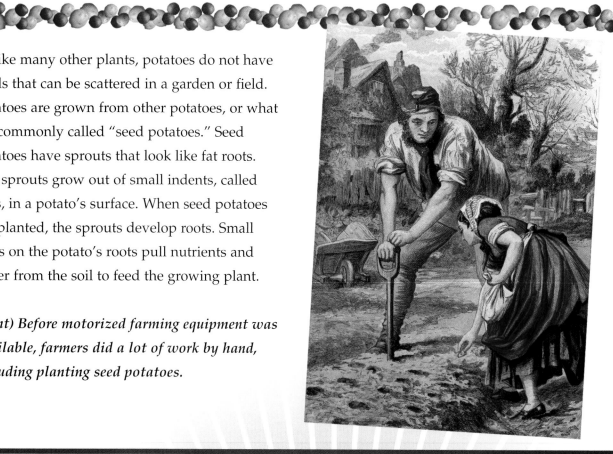

Tuberific!

The potato plant is sometimes called a tuber. What that means is that the plant's fruit, or the potato we eat, grows from an underground stem, called a rhizome. The rhizome is used to store food for the growing plant. Tubers are the swollen fleshy end of a seed potato's rhizomes. On each potato plant, there are several rhizomes, and several tubers, or potatoes.

◄ *Potato plant rhizomes usually grow horizontally underground, and are often between five and 12 inches (13 and 31 centimeters) long.*

Preparing the Fields

Farmers and gardeners must make sure their fields are free of weeds by tilling the soil prior to planting. They also fertilize the soil, often with animal dung or chemical fertilizers, to make the soil rich in nutrients to feed the plants. Potatoes are planted in mounds, or small hills. The mounds protect the early growing potatoes from frost and keep the soil well drained. Commercially grown potatoes are sometimes planted in furrows, or raised rows, in the soil using tractors and other modern equipment. Once the seed potato roots begin to grow underground, green stems and leaves force their way out above the ground.

▸ *This tractor is planting two rows of seed potatoes at once.*

▾ *This potato farm in Japan has dozens of rows of potato plants. The flowers of potato plants are often purple or white.*

Watch them Grow!

It takes about one month from planting for a seed potato to begin to form tubers. The green above-ground stems of the plant also blossom into flowers. Potato plants grow in all kinds of weather conditions, but they grow best with a lot of Sun and water. Most potatoes take between 70 and 140 days, depending on the variety and where they are grown, to grow from a seed potato to a fully mature plant ready for harvesting.

Harvest Time

For thousands of years, potato farmers dug the tubers from the ground at harvest time. Today, commercially grown potatoes are harvested by mechanical pickers. Before the potatoes are harvested, a digging machine lifts the potatoes out of the ground and leaves them on top of the soil in rows. The pickers, or harvesters, then pick up the potatoes, and separate them from any dirt, or debris. The potatoes are then relayed to a truck that is driving alongside the harvester. Harvesting is done in cool, dry weather, to protect the potatoes from diseases and damage caused by warm temperatures. In the northern hemisphere, harvesting is done in the fall, while farmers in the southern hemisphere pick their potatoes in spring.

Potato harvesters are often pieces of equipment that are pulled by tractors.

Storage and Sorting

After harvesting, potato tubers are put into storage warehouses. The warehouses are kept cool and free from excess moisture, which could rot the potatoes. Before the potatoes are sold, they are sorted and graded, or categorized, according to their size and quality. They are usually packaged in thick paper bags, cloth sacks, or plastic, and sold to processors and grocery stores.

Promoting Potatoes

The potato's success throughout the world can be attributed to the fact that the vegetable is nutritious and easily grown. In some countries, growers associations or agencies use advertisements to market, or promote, potatoes to the public. They take out advertisements in newspapers, magazines, and on television that tell how potatoes are nutritious and tasty, in the hopes people will buy more potatoes.

These workers are inspecting potatoes as they travel on a conveyor belt.

Some potatoes are sent to processing plants where they are made into other products, such as French fries.

Ancient Potatoes

The potato has a long history. Botanists, or plant scientists, believe it was cultivated, or farmed, in Peru as far back as 7,000 years ago. The ancient peoples of South America domesticated the wild potatoes that grew in the Andes Mountains. Their knowledge of potato growing was passed on to their **descendants**, the Inca, a powerful people that lived throughout South America from around 1200 to the early 1570s, and later to the descendants of the Inca who still live in the Andes today.

The peoples of Peru still harvest many varieties of potato. If one variety develops disease, they still have other potatoes to harvest.

Ancient Andean Farmers

It is difficult to grow crops on mountainsides because of the steepness and different climates, or weather conditions. For example, sunlight will often beam on one part of a mountain while another part is in shadow, making it dark and cold. Ancient Andean farmers developed thousands of varieties of potatoes that were suited to different climates. Their potatoes came in many sizes, shapes, tastes, and textures. Some potatoes had yellow, red, and orange skins, and others were blue, through and through. They also developed potatoes that could withstand drought and frost without dying.

The Inca Empire

The Inca were an ancient South American people who ruled over a vast territory in the Andes Mountains that included parts of present-day Peru, Ecuador, Bolivia, Chile, and Argentina. The Inca conquered other ancient peoples and incorporated them into an empire that was one of the largest in the ancient world. The Inca built many great cities, and a network of roads linked these cities together. The roads allowed trade to flourish, and gave mountain farmers a route to bring their produce, including potatoes, to market. Potatoes were called *papas* in the Incan Quechua language. The Inca empire lasted for four hundred years, until the Spanish conquered it in the mid-1500s.

(below) Machu Picchu was a city built high up in the mountains by the Inca. Terrace farms surrounded the city.

▼ The Inca believed giving gifts to the god Pachamama, or Mother Earth, would ensure healthy crops. This tradition is upheld by Inca descendants.

Inca Potatoes

Inca farmers did not have tractors or even oxen to plow their fields. They tilled the soil using a long handled foot plow, called a *taclla*. Farmers planted potatoes in the spring and harvested different varieties depending on growing time. Potatoes were an important part of the Incan diet. They were rich in vitamins, including vitamin C, which prevents a body-wasting disease called scurvy. The Inca mashed potatoes to a pulp to remove the water and then set the pulp out in the cold mountain air to freeze dry. Freeze drying was a method of preservation that allowed potatoes to last for years. This way, the Inca could keep aside a store of food in times of poor weather and famine. They used the freeze-dried *papas*, called *chuñu* in stews and to make flat cakes.

*The **taclla** was made of wood and was often as tall, or taller than the person using it.*

In Search of Spices

In the 1400s, Europe was hungry for Asian spices, which were used as medicines and to flavor foods. Europeans began looking for a sailing route that could get them to Asia quickly. Most sailed east, but Christopher Columbus, an explorer sailing for Spain, traveled west. He did not find spices, but in 1492, he did stumble across the **New World** when he landed in the **West Indies**. Columbus claimed parts of the New World for Spain. By the mid-1500s, Spanish conquistadors, or conquerors, set out to find new territory in South America. They were looking for gold and other forms of wealth.

(right) Columbus and other European explorers discovered the New World contained many riches, including potatoes.

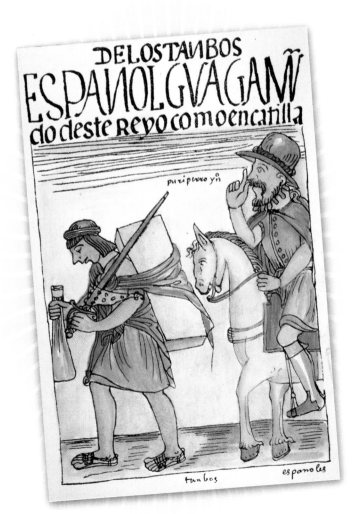

Spanish Conquest

Spanish conquistador Francisco Pizarro changed the lives of the Inca people forever. In 1533, Pizarro and his men traveled through Incan territory on the Pacific coast of Peru. They found the Sapa Inca, or Inca emperor, Atahuallpa, and his soldiers. Atahuallpa was invited to the Spanish camp. When the emperor came, the conquistadors killed his guards and took Atahuallpa captive. Even after a ransom of gold was paid, the Spanish killed the Inca emperor. With no clear leader, the Inca empire fell into disarray and collapsed. Pizarro set up a Spanish colony in Peru, and more colonies were established thoughout South America. Most colonists preferred corn, another vegetable native to the New World. Potatoes were eaten mostly by native South Americans.

◄ *Colonists treated the Inca harshly.*

15

The Potato Spreads

Throughout the mid-1500s, Spanish sailors carried potatoes from South America back across the Atlantic and ate them on the journey. Potatoes helped prevent scurvy, a disease common among sailors who had no fresh fruit or meat to eat while at sea. Historians believe Spanish sailors might have grown potatoes at home. Many of these sailors were Basques, from Northern Spain. Potatoes grew well in Basque country and historians believe they were carried by Basque fishermen and sailors to other areas of the world, including Ireland. The Spanish also introduced the potato to the rest of Europe.

When potatoes were spreading across Europe, most farmers were growing wheat.

Cool Reception

At first, many Europeans did not want to plant or eat potatoes because they were afraid of them. Potatoes belong to the same family as a poisonous plant called deadly nightshade, and many people thought they were poisonous. Europeans were used to eating grains such as wheat, which they made into flour for breads. Most of the farmland was used to plant wheat. Potatoes were a food only eaten by the very poor, partly because they were inexpensive and easy to grow. Potatoes proved good at keeping the poor from starving. With less people starving, the population grew. Over time, potatoes became known as lifesavers.

Famine

Europe had many famines, or severe shortages of food, from the 1300s through the 1800s. Most of the farmland in Europe was used to grow wheat. Poor weather or wars that prevented farmers from seeding or harvesting wheat, often resulted in famine. Without enough food, people slowly starved to death. They developed diseases caused by malnutrition, or not getting enough nutrients they needed from their diets. Farmers often ate their seed crops, such as wheat, during famines, and killed and ate their **draft animals** just to survive. This left them without the means to farm. When wheat harvests failed, the price of wheat products, such as grain, flour, and bread, went up. Riots broke out in the streets of cities where people fought for food.

Famine Fighters

The potato became an important famine fighter, particularly during times of war. In the 1600s and 1700s, a time of many European wars, armies spent months traveling overland. The armies pillaged, or robbed, villages along the way, taking crops to feed themselves. Unlike wheat, potatoes grew underground and, while soldiers would take the villager's wheat and stored grain, they did not dig up their potatoes. As a nutritious and available food source, potatoes helped villagers fight starvation.

World War I, a conflict that took place mostly in Europe between 1914 and 1918, was also a time of food shortages. These German people are exchanging potato peels for firewood. The peels were made into other foods, such as soups.

Parmentier: Potato Promoter

The potato might never have become a diet staple in Europe if not for French apothecary, or pharmacist, Antoine-Augustin Parmentier. Parmentier was serving in the French army during the **Seven Years War** from 1756 to 1763. He was taken prisoner by **Prussia**. While prisoner, Parmentier was fed only potatoes. He managed to not only survive, but thrive on the diet. In the 1780s, he convinced the king of France that potatoes should be grown throughout France. The French, like most Europeans at the time, thought potatoes were poisonous, or animal food at best. The king gave Parmentier land to grow potatoes. Parmentier made sure the king's soldiers guarded the crop by day, but left at night so nearby farmers would become curious, thinking the potatoes must be precious if guarded by the king's soldiers. Parmentier's plan worked, and the crop was soon stolen. The French came to love potatoes and they became a big part of French cuisine.

▲ *The name "Parmentier" is used for many potato dishes, including* **Hachis Parmentier,** *or shepherd's pie, which has a top layer of mashed potato.*

(below) Parmentier hosted dinners for nobles where potatoes were served for every food course from soup to dessert.

18

Spud Salvation

When early European agronomists, or crop scientists, learned of the potato's ability to keep peasants alive during famines, they began urging more peasant farmers to grow potatoes. Unlike wheat, potatoes were not a commodity, sold to make a profit. Potatoes were simply fuel for life, that supplied people with an inexpensive way to stay healthy. Kings and governments throughout Europe urged and **decreed** that their people should plant potatoes, and rely less on bread. Eventually, people complied and the potato became a common vegetable in many parts of Europe.

▲ *Frederick the Great, king of Prussia (1712 to 1786), issued a decree that his subjects grow potatoes, believing potatoes would solve the problem of food shortages.*

▶ *Potatoes were brought to Egypt by the British who colonized the area in the 1800s. Today, Egypt is one of the largest producers of potatoes in Africa.*

Colonies Built on Potatoes

Potatoes also spread to other areas of the world when colonies were established. A colony is a territory under the control of another country. The aim of the colonizer was often to extract riches, such as gold, minerals, or agricultural products, from the colony to bring them back to the colonizing country. Settlers came from the colonizing country to set up farms and businesses in the colony. The settlers brought plants, animals, and ways of doing things from their home country to the colony. Potatoes were one plant taken from a New World colony, in this case Peru, and brought back to Europe. Throughout the 1800s and early 1900s, when the countries of Europe colonized much of Asia, Africa, and the South Pacific, the potato was the one dependable vegetable that colonizers brought with them. They were grown in kitchen gardens and over time became important food crops for the local peoples as well.

The Potato and Ireland

The potato was first brought to Ireland in the mid-1500s. It adapted well to the moist climate and boggy soils of Ireland. By the 1800s it had become a staple crop for Irish peasant farmers.

English Control

There was already a long history of English control over Ireland by the time the potato arrived. Ireland was conquered and reconquered and over time, the Irish had their lands taken from them and given to English landlords. When the Irish revolted against this, they were punished. Laws were passed, allowing terrible **discrimination** against the Irish and even more of their land was taken away. English landlords set up large farming estates.

▲ *Irish people were poor during English rule.*

Ireland is on an island in the north Atlantic Ocean. Its rolling hills and rich soils are ideal for farming and pastureland, where sheep and cattle graze.

Tenant Farmers

The Irish became tenant farmers of the English landlords, on land that was once their own. They lived on small plots of land and paid rents to the landlords. They grew wheat, oats, and other crops and raised pigs and cattle, all for export, or shipment, to England. The food they grew for export paid the rents on their plots of land. They grew potatoes to feed themselves. The Irish tenant farmers had no rights to the land they farmed. They could be evicted at any time. Their homes were crude, window-less mud sheds. The tenant farmers also shared their land with other landless workers who helped farm the land in turn for a place to live and a small area to plant their own potatoes. The tenant farming system made nearly all Irish dependent on the potato for survival.

Food of the Peasants

In the 1800s, the Irish ate a simple diet of potatoes and milk that supplied them with all their nutritional needs. They grew the potatoes for themselves on their small plots. An acre of potatoes could feed a family for a year. The potato grown most frequently in Ireland at this time was called the lumper because it was big and lumpy.

(above) Irish tenant farmers often lived in crude, one room cottages, or sheds. If they made improvements to their homes, their rent was increased or their homes were taken away from them by their landlords. If Irish tenants fell behind in their rent, they were evicted and made homeless. Everyone feared becoming homeless.

The Great Hunger

In 1845, a sudden and fast moving potato disease, or blight, called *Phytophthora infestans*, made its way through Ireland. The blight was an airborne **fungus** carried by the wind. It caused potatoes to blacken and rot into a stinking mess. The blight spread quickly, and destroyed crops within days. Even potatoes already dug from the ground and stored, rotted. With their only food crop ruined, the Irish began to starve.

◄ *Irish children scoured, or searched, fields for edible potatoes during the famine.*

Dead and Dying

The landowners and government believed the blight would be short-lived and refused to offer help. When great numbers of people began to die, the **British government**, which controlled Ireland, brought **rations** of corn meal to Ireland. When the rations ran out, people began to starve again. The blight killed the potato crop for three more years. People across Ireland starved while Irish grain, cattle, and pigs were exported to England. Irish tenant farmers had to sell the grain and animals to pay their rents and avoid being evicted. The desperately poor and starving Irish rioted at ports where the grain and animals were being loaded on to ships. The British responded by sending troops to protect the grain, but no **relief** to keep the starving Irish from dying.

(above) Potato blight affects the plants' leaves, stems, and tubers.

Ships of Immigration

An estimated one million Irish, of a population of eight million, died from the famine and famine-related diseases from 1845 to 1849. Up to two million more left Ireland on **immigration** ships. Most were bound for England, North America, and Australia. The ships became known as coffin ships because so many Irish died of starvation and disease, such as **typhus**, during the passage. Landlords who evicted tenant farmers often packed their tenants off in coffin ships and began using their land to raise cattle. For a time during the famine, the British set up a weak plan of relief, including road building programs to give Irish people work. Even when the blight no longer affected potatoes, food shortages and hunger continued for many years.

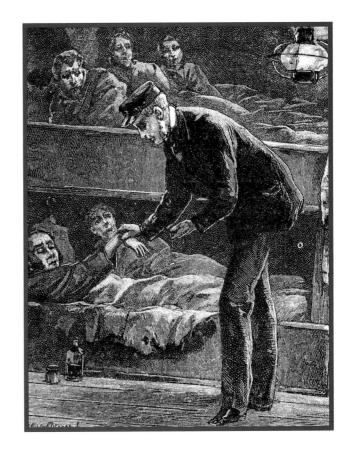

▼ *Today, potatoes are still a major crop grown throughout Ireland.*

An Gorta Mor

The Irish call the potato famine the great hunger, or *an gorta mor*, in the Irish Gaelic language. They believe it was more than just a failure of a crop, but also an example of how a people were nearly wiped out by colonial oppression, or unjust treatment by a foreign ruler. The famine devastated Ireland for many years. Entire areas of the country were **depopulated**, and many Irish continued to move to other countries well into the mid-1900s. It took over 100 years for Ireland's **economy** to recover from *an gorta mor*.

(above) Many Irish immigrants were quarantined once they arrived at their destinations.

Back to the New World

The potato was brought to North America in the early 1700s by Irish immigrants. It did not take long before potatoes were grown throughout North America. Thomas Jefferson, the third president of the United States, was known to have grown many new and unusual plants in his gardens. Potatoes were one such plant. He kept diaries on how the potato plant grew, and noted that he enjoyed eating potatoes from his garden.

Some areas of Idaho are dry so irrigation systems, such as sprinkler systems, supply water to the potato crops.

Potato Growing Centers

Over time, farmers in many areas of North America began growing potatoes as commercial crops. Potatoes were also sold to settlers moving west across America. Idaho, a state in the northwestern United States, has rich soil, and warm days and cool nights in the growing season, making it a perfect place for growing potatoes. The Idaho potato **industry** began to really grow in the late 1800s, when American **horticulturist** Luther Burbank developed a disease resistant potato. Today, Idaho is the center of American potato production and the Russet Burbank is still the main variety. Other top potato growing states include Washington, Maine, Oregon, Wisconsin, and North Dakota.

Prince Edward Island

Prince Edward Island (PEI), a small Canadian island province in the Atlantic Ocean near Nova Scotia and New Brunswick, has long been the country's potato capital. Potatoes have been grown there since the late 1700s and the island even has the nickname of Spud Island. Farmers in PEI grow potatoes for the seed market as well as for food processing and grocery store produce aisles. Potatoes grow well in Prince Edward Island's rich red soil and temperate climate. New Brunswick is also a major Canadian potato producer. Together, the two provinces produce 87 percent of the country's seed potatoes. Ontario and Quebec are also major potato producing provinces.

A trusting farmer sells potatoes in PEI. His sign says, "Please make your change from the box. Thanks."

Prince Edward Island is famous for its rich red soil, and the delicious potatoes that grow in it.

Diseases and Threats

Potatoes were first cultivated thousands of years ago. Since that time, many different varieties, or types, have developed. The potatoes brought to Europe by the Spanish were of just a few varieties. Over hundreds of years of commercial cultivation, potatoes have become more susceptible, or vulnerable, to disease and insects.

This farmer's crop has experienced drought conditions. The potatoes he holds should be twice as big.

Potato Pests and Diseases

As long as there has been plants, there have been pests. Thousands of years ago, before many plants were **domesticated**, plants and pests both changed in natural reaction to each other. Plants developed resistances to the insects that fed on them, such as becoming bitter in taste. In turn, the insects developed immunity, or ways to protect themselves, against the plant's resistance. This was a natural process that went back and forth and continued after plants were domesticated.

Potato blight still affects potato plants today.

The larvae, or young, of potato beetles damage leaves by feeding on them.

Chemical Weapons

Today, commercial farmers fight pests and diseases with chemical pesticides to control insects, diseases, and fungi in the soil, such as the fungus that destroyed Irish crops during the famine. They also use herbicides to rid fields of weeds. Farmers spend thousands of dollars a year trying to keep their crops from being destroyed by diseases and insects. These chemicals must be used under strict safety conditions because they can be harmful to health. Farmers should always wear protective clothing and masks. Some scientists believe some chemical pesticides and herbicides can cause cancer. These chemicals can also seep into **groundwater** and pollute waterways in the area.

(right) Some pesticides are released from planes.

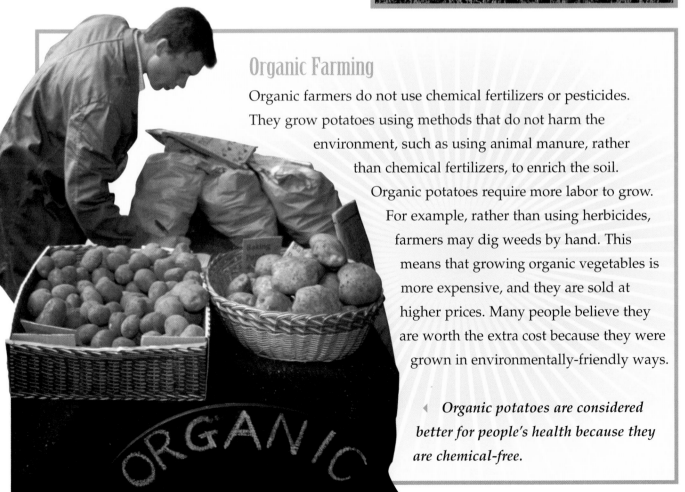

Organic Farming

Organic farmers do not use chemical fertilizers or pesticides. They grow potatoes using methods that do not harm the environment, such as using animal manure, rather than chemical fertilizers, to enrich the soil. Organic potatoes require more labor to grow. For example, rather than using herbicides, farmers may dig weeds by hand. This means that growing organic vegetables is more expensive, and they are sold at higher prices. Many people believe they are worth the extra cost because they were grown in environmentally-friendly ways.

◀ *Organic potatoes are considered better for people's health because they are chemical-free.*

From Tubers to Fries

Once potatoes became accepted and established in a place, they were adapted to the local cuisines, or styles of cooking. The Irish are still partial to potatoes, and few Irish meals are served without them. Potatoes are incredibly versatile and can be eaten boiled, baked, steamed, fried, mashed, and in baked goods and treats.

▲ *French fries are believed to have been invented in Belgium, where they are known as* **pomme frites,** *and are served with mayonnaise.*

Potato Lore

Potatoes were more than a food to the ancient Andean farmers who first cultivated them. They were also a medicine. The high levels of vitamin C in potatoes helped prevent scurvy. Later European lore about the potato ranged from the strange to downright wacky. People believed that rubbing a cut potato on a wart and then burying the potato in the ground would get rid of the wart. They also believed that carrying a potato in your pocket could cure a toothache, and that pregnant women should avoid potatoes because eating them would cause their babies to be born with big heads.

◄ *Potatoes have become a part of North American culture. There are toys and counting games about potatoes. Potato sack races are held at parties and picnics, and people who sit around watching a lot of television are called couch potatoes.*

Chips and Crisps

There are many stories about where the first potato chip was made. Some say chips, or crisps as they are known in Britain, had their start at a restaurant in Saratoga Springs, New York. The chef there had prepared French fries for a customer. When they were rejected twice as too thick, the frustrated chef fried up the thinnest slices he could. To his surprise, the customer loved them and soon others asked for them. In the 1920s, a traveling salesperson named Herman Lay began selling thin, crisply fried potato chips to customers throughout the southern United States. Eventually Lay bought out his employer and started his own business, the H. W. Lay Company. Lay's company became Frito-Lay, one of the first big snack food companies.

▸ *Lay's chips come in many flavors, including dill pickle, pizza, and the original salted variety.*

Starch my Collar

Potato starch is a fine flour-like substance produced by crushing potatoes and collecting the juice, or "starch milk," and drying it out. Potato starch is used in cooking and baking. It is a natural thickener used in gravies and other sauces. Starch is also used as an edible coating to preserve some perishable foods, such as nuts, and as paper and textile coating, which makes the products more durable. Starch production is a multi-million dollar industry.

(left) This photograph was taken in 1910 and used the autochrome process. Autochrome photography used potato starch grains to fix colored dyes to glass plates.

The Potato's Future

Potatoes are versatile plants. They are still grown in yards and gardens to feed families, and also on large commercial farms. Most commercial farms grow only a few varieties of potatoes to suit the climate they are grown in and to serve major buyers, such as grocery stores and processors. Grocery stores in North America rarely sell more than four types of potatoes. Large processors buy the variety of potatoes that suits their purpose. For instance, fast food chain restaurants may want a large, firm, and starchy potato. Since they buy hundreds of thousands of potatoes a year, growers will plant only the type of potato buyers want. Growing just one variety or type of crop is called monoculture. Some scientists believe monoculture forces large-scale farmers to use more pesticides, since fields of the same plant are more likely to be wiped out if they become prey to insects and diseases.

Heritage Potatoes

Some smaller farmers still grow what is known today as "heritage varieties." Heritage varieties are potatoes that have long histories, or varieties that were grown hundreds, or even thousands of years ago. Growing heritage varieties preserves the diversity of potatoes. Diversity, or a lot of variety, means that there is less chance that potatoes will be wiped out by disease and that there will always be different kinds of potatoes for different growing conditions. It also helps to ensure that the early varieties do not die out, because they are not being grown anymore.

About 300 million tons (272 million tonnes) of potatoes are harvested each year. One third of that harvest now comes from developing countries. Developing countries are less wealthy, and many people in developing countries work in agriculture, or farming.

Bioengineered Potatoes

Bioengineered potatoes are potatoes that have been genetically altered, or modified, to make them resistant to pests or diseases or to improve their taste or lengthen their shelf life. In bioengineering, the **genes** of other plants, animals, or chemicals are introduced into the potato's genes. Many people believe bioengineered foods could be harmful to humans because it is fairly new and no one knows the long-term effects. Many farmers do not want to grow bioengineered potatoes because major buyers, such as fast food restaurants, do not want to use them. In India, one of the world's biggest potato growers, a genetically modified potato called the "protato" has been promoted as a way to stamp out malnutrition. The protato has been genetically altered to contain more **protein**. Critics have said the protato is not as full of protein as many other traditional Indian foods, such as beans, and the promotion of protato is a ploy to make money.

▲ *Some restaurants are wary of making foods, including French fries, from bioengineered potatoes.*

International Potato Center

Imagine an entire organization devoted to improving the potato and other tubers! The International Potato Center (or CIP in Spanish) researches potato growth, use, and markets throughout the world. The center's focus is on reducing poverty and promoting potatoes as a nutritious, dependable food, particularly in poorer areas of the world. The center is located in Peru, the ancestral home of the potato and it is funded by donor governments, museums, and aid agencies throughout the world. The CIP conducts research on potato genetics, growing potatoes in new areas, combating blight, and improving yields.

◀ *The International Potato Center has a data bank of different potato species, including wild Andean varieties.*

Glossary

Andes Mountains A mountain chain that runs along the west coast of South America

biodegradable Materials that can decompose

British government The government of England, Wales, Scotland, and at the time, all of Ireland

carbohydrate A plant substance that animals and people use for food

commercial Relating to businesses, or buying and selling products

conquer To defeat or control by force

decree An order coming from a high authority

depopulate A decrease in a population

descendants People connected by blood to other peoples

discrimination Unfair treatment based on prejudice

domesticated Began farming a wild plant

draft animal An animal used to pull loads

economy Money and business that comes in and out of a country and provides jobs for the people

fungus A plant-like organism, including mushrooms and molds

genes Information in cells of a plant or animal that create the specific features of the organism

groundwater A store of water underground

horticulturist Scientists that specialize in the growing of fruits, vegetables, and flowers

immigration Moving to another country

industry Businesses that take part in a field of work, such as the farming industry

New World North, South, and Central America

nobles People of high position in society

nutritious Full of goodness

plunder Using force to steal goods

processors Companies that make products using different materials

protein A nutrient people need to stay healthy

Prussia A former kingdom, or territory, in present-day Germany and Poland

quarantine To isolate because of illness

ration A small amount of food, given out during food shortages

relief A plan to help those in need

Seven Years War A war that took place in Europe between 1756 and 1763

temperate A region with mild temperatures

tropical A region with hot and humid weather

typhus A disease causing rash, fever, and confusion; often transmitted by lice and fleas

West Indies The islands, also called the Caribbean, between the Caribbean Sea and the Atlantic Ocean

Index

Printed in the U.S.A.